BREAKFAST EXPRESS

Fast, Healthy Breakfast Recipes in 10 Minutes Or Less!

By Dan DeFigio

Other books by this author:

    Beating Sugar Addiction For Dummies

    The Two Week Transformation

    Beach Games For Kids!

    Beyond Smoothies

    Princess Wiggly

BREAKFAST EXPRESS

© 2018 Iron Ring Publishing.

All rights reserved. Printed in the United States of America.

No part of this publication or the information it contains may be quoted, reused, transmitted, or reproduced in any form – electronic, mechanical, photocopy, recording, or otherwise – without prior written permission of the copyright holder, except in the case of brief quotations embodied in critical articles or reviews.

For information contact IronRingPublishing.com

ISBN: 978-1791337810

First Edition: December 2018

10 9 8 7 6 5 4 3 2 1

BREAKFAST EXPRESS

FAST healthy breakfasts in 10 minutes or less!

Table of Contents (Alphabetical)

Bacon and Eggs in Avocado Halves (Paleo) 16

Bacon-Banana Frittata in a Mug (Paleo) 18

Banana Bread Quick (Paleo, Vegan, Gluten-Free) 20

Banana Pancake (Gluten-Free) 22

Breakfast Salad (Paleo) 24

Breakfast Sandwich with Cheese and Veggies (Vegetarian) 26

Cherry Yogurt Breakfast in a Glass (Vegetarian) 28

Cinnamon-Maple Oatmeal with Raisins (Gluten-Free, Vegetarian) 30

Egg and Cottage Cheese Sandwich 32

Egg in Bacon-Lattice Bun (Paleo) 34

Egg Quesadilla 36

Eggs, Sausage, and Hash Browns (Gluten-Free) 38

English Muffin (Paleo, Gluten-Free) 40

Fruity Flaxseed Smoothie (Gluten-Free, Vegan) 42

Granola Mug (Gluten-Free, Vegan) 44

Green Smoothie (Gluten-Free, Vegetarian) 46

Ham and Egg Bowl (Gluten-Free) 48

Microwave Scrambled Egg Mug (Gluten-Free) 50

Power Chocolate Smoothie (Paleo, Gluten-Free) 52

Quinoa Porridge with Fruit (Gluten-Free, Vegetarian) 54

Scrambled Tofu with Turmeric (Gluten-Free, Vegetarian) 56

Smoothie Bowl with Fruit (Vegetarian) 58

Spicy Scrambled Eggs with Dates (Paleo, Gluten-Free) 60

Spinach Ricotta Scramble (Gluten-Free) 62

Strawberry-Yogurt Waffles (Vegetarian) 64

Superfood Breakfast Bowl (Gluten-Free, Vegetarian) 66

Turkey and Cheese Scramble (Gluten-Free) 68

Turkey Sausage, Egg, and Fruit (Paleo, Gluten-Free) 70

Veggie Stir-Fry with Eggs (Paleo) 72

Zucchini Power Omelet (Paleo) 74

ABOUT THE AUTHOR 76

Other books from IronRingPublishing.com:
The Two Week Transformation 78
Beyond Smoothies 80

Disclaimer and Terms of Use 82

PALEO Fast Breakfast Listing:

Bacon and Eggs in Avocado Halves (Paleo)..........16

Bacon-Banana Frittata in a Mug (Paleo)...............18

Banana Bread Quick (Paleo, Vegan, Gluten-Free)..20

Breakfast Salad (Paleo)...24

Egg in Bacon-Lattice Bun (Paleo).......................34

English Muffin (Paleo, Gluten-Free)......................40

Power Chocolate Smoothie (Paleo, Gluten-Free)..52

Spicy Scrambled Eggs with Dates (Paleo, Gluten-Free)..60

Turkey Sausage, Egg, and Fruit (Paleo, Gluten-Free)..70

Veggie Stir-Fry with Eggs (Paleo)...........................72

Zucchini Power Omlette (Paleo).............................74

GLUTEN-FREE Fast Breakfast Listing:

Banana Bread Quick (Paleo, Vegan, Gluten-Free)..20

Banana Pancake (Gluten-Free).................................22

Cinnamon-Maple Oatmeal with Raisins (Gluten-Free)..30

Eggs, Sausage, and Hash Browns (Gluten-Free).38

English Muffin (Paleo, Gluten-Free).................40

Fruity Flaxseed Smoothie (Gluten-Free, Vegan)..42

Granola Mug (Gluten-Free, Vegan).........................44

Green Smoothie (Gluten-Free, Vegetarian).........46

Ham and Egg Bowl (Gluten-Free).............................48

Microwave Scrambled Egg Mug (Gluten-Free)...50

Power Chocolate Smoothie (Paleo, Gluten-Free)..52

Quinoa Porridge with Fruit (Gluten-Free, Vegetarian)..54

Scrambled Tofu with Turmeric (Gluten-Free, Vegetarian)..56

Spicy Scrambled Eggs with Dates (Paleo, Gluten-Free)..60

GLUTEN-FREE Fast Breakfast Listing (continued):

Spinach Ricotta Scramble (Gluten-Free)...............62

Superfood Breakfast Bowl (Gluten-Free, Vegetarian)..66

Turkey and Cheese Scramble (Gluten-Free).......68

Turkey Sausage, Egg, and Fruit (Paleo, Gluten-Free)..66

VEGETARIAN Fast Breakfast Listing:

Note: In Breakfast Express, the category of "vegetarian" indicates that the recipe does not contain meat, fish, or egg products. It may contain dairy.

Please read through the ingredient list carefully to ensure that your fast breakfasts comply with your dietary preferences.

Banana Bread Quick (Paleo, Vegan, Gluten-Free)..20

Breakfast Sandwich with Cheese and Veggies (Vegetarian)..26

Cherry Yogurt Breakfast in a Glass (Vegetarian)..28

Cinnamon-Maple Oatmeal with Raisins (Gluten-Free, Vegetarian)......................................30

Fruity Flaxseed Smoothie (Gluten-Free, Vegan)..42

Granola Mug (Gluten-Free, Vegan)........................44

Green Smoothie (Gluten-Free, Vegetarian).........42

VEGETARIAN Fast Breakfast Listing (continued):

Quinoa Porridge with Fruit (Gluten-Free, Vegetarian)..................50

Scrambled Tofu with Turmeric (Gluten-Free, Vegetarian)..................52

Smoothie Bowl with Fruit (Vegetarian)..................54

Strawberry-Yogurt Waffles (Vegetarian)..............60

Superfood Breakfast Bowl (Gluten-Free, Vegetarian)..................62

INTRODUCTION

People who skip breakfast are more than four times as likely to be obese than people who eat something in the morning.
(American Journal of Epidemiology)

Research shows that between 35% and 40% of all Americans skip breakfast, and many kids leave for school without it.

The #1 reason that people give for not eating breakfast is NO TIME.

Solution: Breakfast Express is here to give you dozens of healthy breakfasts that you can put together FAST!

What constitutes a good breakfast?

1. Natural foods.

Natural foods contain nutrients and fiber, but are free from chemicals and other additives. Even if you are into the bacon-heavy Paleo lifestyle, you should always seek out bacon that is uncured and free from nitrites, smoke flavoring, and other unhealthy chemicals.

Eggs from pasture-raised chickens are more nutritious than eggs from industrial farms.

Whenever possible, stick to vegetables, fruits, unprocessed grains, nuts, organic meats and eggs, hormone-free dairy, and pure whey protein without additives.

2. Get some protein.

Higher protein breakfasts translate into a more sustained level of energy throughout the morning. Protein fills you up longer, and you're less likely to have midmorning cravings. You're also less likely to overeat at lunch, or to be so hungry that you'll grab whatever takeout garbage you can get your hands on.

And higher protein at breakfast increases your metabolism: In one study, a high-protein breakfast increased the metabolism of healthy young women by a shocking 100%!

Numerous studies over the years have shown that skipping breakfast impacts the behavior and mental performance of school kids: Kids who eat breakfast have better memory, and higher math and reading scores. And kids who are hungry have a large number of behavior problems, including fighting, stealing, having difficulty with teachers and not acknowledging rules.

3. Don't eat the same thing every day.

People who eat breakfast are far more likely to get a healthy intake of vitamins and minerals than those who skip breakfast. In one study published in the *Journal of the American College of Nutrition*, researchers found that people who ate a healthy breakfast containing more than one-quarter of their daily calories had a higher intake of essential vitamins and minerals, and lower cholesterol levels to boot.

One of the easiest ways to ensure that you get the wide variety of nutrients that is essential for optimal health: Mix up your menus! Take advantage of the multitude of recipes in this collection to make your breakfast not only FAST, but NOT BORING.

FAST BREAKFAST RECIPES

Bacon and Eggs in Avocado Halves (Paleo)

Yield: 2 servings

Ingredients

2 strips bacon, organic, sugar- and nitrate-free
1 avocado, halved
2 pasture-raised eggs
Salt and pepper, to taste
Chili or paprika, to taste (optional)

Directions

1. Wrap bacon on paper towels and place in a microwavable plate. Cook in microwave at 70% power for 2-3 minutes.
2. Remove the stone from the avocado and scoop out some of the flesh to make space for the eggs. Fill the halves with 1 egg each and season with salt, pepper and chili or paprika (if using). Cook in the microwave 30 seconds at a time until whites are opaque (2 minutes).
3. Sprinkle with chopped or crumbled bacon.

Nutrition Information

Serving size: 1 egg-filled avocado half
Calories: 303
Total Fat: 24.3 g
Total Carbohydrate: 8 g
Sugars: 0.4 g
Protein: 15.1 g
Sodium: 548 mg

Bacon-Banana Frittata in a Mug (Paleo)

Yield: 1 serving

Ingredients

2 eggs
Pinch of salt
1 Tablespoon coconut oil
1/2 ripe banana
1 piece of crumbled cooked bacon (organic, nitrate- and sugar-free)

Directions

1. Put eggs, salt, coconut oil and banana in a blender and pulse until smooth (30 seconds).
2. Place in a mug and cook in microwave on HIGH for 30 seconds. Stir and then microwave another 1-2 minutes until egg sets.
3. Sprinkle with crumbled bacon.

Optional: Add fresh chopped vegetables, like broccoli, spinach, and/or tomato between steps 1 and 2.

Nutrition Information

Serving size: 1 mug
Calories: 370
Total Fat: 26.9 g
Total Carbohydrate: 14.3 g
Sugars: 7.6 g
Protein: 16.8 g
Sodium: 596 mg

Banana Bread Quick (Paleo, Vegan, Gluten-Free)

Yield: 1 serving

Ingredients

1/2 medium overripe banana, mashed
Dash of cinnamon
1 Tablespoon coconut flour
1 Tablespoon almond butter or any nut butter of choice
2 Tablespoons coconut milk
Chopped nuts or dairy-free chocolate chips (optional)

Directions

1. In a small bowl, mix together mashed banana, cinnamon, coconut flour and nut butter, blending well.
2. Add milk gradually, mixing well.
3. Add nuts or chocolate chips, if using.
4. Add to a microwave-proof mug, ramekin or bowl.
5. Bake in microwave for 50-60 seconds, depending on your microwave and the texture you want.

Nutrition Information

Serving size: 1 piece
Calories: 192
Total Fat: 10.5 g
Total Carbohydrate: 23 g
Sugars: 8.7 g
Protein: 4.2 g
Sodium: 7mg

Banana Pancake (Gluten-Free)

Yield: 1 serving

Ingredients

1-2 teaspoons coconut oil
1 ripe banana
1/2 cup rolled oats
2 eggs
2 Tablespoons apple sauce
A dash of cinnamon

Directions

1. Heat oil in a pan over medium heat.
2. Place the rest of the ingredients in a blender and blend well (30 seconds).
3. Pour the batter into the pan dividing to make about 3 large pancakes.
4. Cook until browned on both sides (about 1-2 minutes per side)
5. Good with fruit or nut butter.

Nutrition Information

Serving size: 3 pancakes
Calories: 451
Total Fat: 17.5 g
Total Carbohydrate: x g
Sugars: 18.7 g
Protein: 18.9 g
Sodium: 144 mg

Breakfast Salad (Paleo)

Yield: 2 servings

Ingredients
2 Tablespoons grass-fed butter
4 pasture-raised eggs
4 cups greens of choice (spinach, kale, turnip, chard, bok choi, arugula), washed
1 cup cherry tomatoes, halved
2 Tablespoons onion, chopped
Juice of 1 lemon
1-2 Tablespoons extra virgin olive oil
Dried or fresh oregano, to taste
Salt and pepper, to taste
1 oz Bacon pieces (no added sugar or chemicals), or 1 oz chopped breakfast ham

Directions

1. Put the butter in a pan and place over medium high heat to melt.
2. Drop the eggs into pan.
3. Place lid and let the eggs cook.
4. Meanwhile, combine vegetables, lemon juice, oil and seasoning.
5. Top with cooked eggs.
6. Sprinkle with bacon bits or ham. Also delicious with some added fresh strawberries!

Nutrition Information (without adding fruit)

Serving size: 2 1/2 cups
Calories: 323
Total Fat: 30.7 g
Total Carbohydrate: 6.8 g
Sugars: 2 g
Protein: 8 g
Sodium: 315 mg

Breakfast Sandwich with Cheese and Veggies (Vegetarian)

Yield: 1 serving

Ingredients
1/2 cup chopped spinach leaves
1 Tablespoon red onion, finely sliced
1/2 cup liquid egg substitute
1 whole wheat muffin
1 slice Swiss cheese
Non-stick cooking spray

Directions

1. Spray a microwave-safe mug or bowl, about the same diameter as the sandwich bun, with non-stick cooking spray.
2. Place the spinach and onion inside and heat in cook in microwave until spinach is wilted (about 1 minute).
3. Add egg substitute. Beat a little and cook for 30 seconds.
4. Stir briefly and return to cook another 1 minute or until set.
5. Make a sandwich with cooked veggie-egg mixture topped with cheese as filling.
6. Heat in microwave to melt cheese (about 20 seconds).

Tip: For a non-vegetarian version, substitute real egg.

Nutrition Information
Serving size: 1 sandwich
Calories: 228
Total Fat: 4 g
Total Carbohydrate: 26.5 g
Sugars: 4.5 g
Protein: 22 g
Sodium: 764 mg

Cherry Yogurt Breakfast in a Glass (Vegetarian)

Yield: 1 serving

Ingredients

1/2 cup unsweetened Greek yogurt
2 Tablespoons milk, soy milk, almond milk, or coconut milk
1 scoop vanilla protein powder
Dash cinnamon
1 1/2 teaspoons chia seeds
3/4 cup fresh or frozen pitted cherries, chopped
Almond slivers, for garnish

Directions

1. Mix yogurt, milk, protein powder, and cinnamon together in a mug or jar until smooth.
2. Stir in chia seeds and cherries.
3. Top with almond slivers.

Nutrition Information

Serving size: 1 1/2 cups
Calories: 268
Total Fat: 6.5 g
Total Carbohydrate: 29 g
Sugars: 21 g
Protein: 26.5 g
Sodium: 100 mg

Cinnamon-Maple Oatmeal with Raisins (Gluten-Free, Vegetarian)

Yield: 1 serving

Ingredients
1/2 cup gluten-free oats
1 cup water
1 scoop whey protein, unflavored or vanilla
2 Tablespoons raisins
1 Tablespoon maple syrup
Dash of cinnamon

Directions

1. Place oats and water in a microwavable bowl with lid.
2. Add cinnamon and mix well.
3. Cover and microwave on high until oats are tender (1-2 minutes).
4. Add raisins, whey protein, and maple syrup.
5. Stir well, reheat 20-30 seconds.
6. Serve warm.

Tip: Also delicious and nutrition with a handful of chopped walnuts or pecans!

Nutrition Information

Serving size: 1 bowl
Calories: 320
Total Fat: 3 g
Total Carbohydrate: 70 g
Sugars: 37.4 g
Protein: 14 g
Sodium: 8 mg

Egg and Cottage Cheese Sandwich

Yield: 1 serving

Ingredients
1 egg, hardboiled
1 whole wheat English muffin, sliced
1/2 cup cottage cheese

Directions
1. Toast bread slices.
2. Spread cottage cheese on both slices and top with sliced boiled egg.
3. Optional: Add some fresh tomato or avocado!

Nutrition Information
Serving size: 1 sandwich
Calories: 292
Total Fat: 7.2 g
Total Carbohydrate: 32.3 g
Sugars: 7.2 g
Protein: 27.1 g
Sodium: 692 mg

Egg in Bacon-Lattice Bun (Paleo)

Yield: 1 serving

Ingredients
6 slices of nitrite-free turkey bacon, each halved crosswise (in equal lengths)
1 Tablespoon coconut oil
2 eggs
1 Tablespoon green onion, chopped

Directions

1. With 3 horizontal half-strips and 3 vertical half-strips, weave into two bacon lattices.
2. Wrap bacon in paper towels and place in a microwavable plate. Cook in microwave at 70% power for 2-3 minutes.
3. Heat oil in a frying pan and fry eggs to desired doneness (3-5 minutes).
4. Sprinkle eggs with green onion and place between 2 bacon-lattice pieces.

Nutrition Information
Serving size: 1 "sandwich"
Calories: 388
Total Fat: 27 g
Total Carbohydrate: 1.4 g
Sugars: 0.3 g
Protein: 32.5 g
Sodium: 1099 mg

Egg Quesadilla

Yield: 1 serving

Ingredients
1/2 Tablespoon butter
2 eggs
1 whole wheat tortilla, warmed
1/4 cup shredded Monterey Jack cheese
1 Tablespoon salsa
1 Tablespoon sour cream (optional)

Directions

1. Melt butter in a frying pan over medium heat.
2. Scramble eggs.
3. Place scrambled eggs on tortilla.
4. Sprinkle with cheese and top with salsa. Optional: add a Tablespoon of sour cream with the salsa.
5. Fold over and cut into slices. You may need to microwave each piece 20-30 seconds to melt the cheese more.

Nutrition Information

Serving size: 1 quesadilla
Calories: 437
Total Fat: 17.9 g
Total Carbohydrate: 24.9 g
Sugars: 3.3 g
Protein: 25 g
Sodium: 760 mg

Eggs, Sausage, and Hash Browns (Gluten-Free)

Yield: 1 serving

Ingredients
2 oz gluten-free chicken or turkey breakfast sausage
1 Tablespoon butter
1 medium russet potato, peeled
Salt and pepper, to taste
1 teaspoon olive or coconut oil, or as needed

Directions

1. Place sausage over 2 paper towels on a microwave-safe plate.
2. Microwave until sausage is warmed through (50-90 seconds).
3. Heat butter in a pan over medium heat.
4. Grate 1/2 of the potato directly in the pan, spreading the shreds into a thin layer.
5. Sprinkle with salt and pepper to taste.
6. When bottom of hash has browned (about 1 minute), flip over and brown other side (1 minute).
7. Place sausage in pan to sear surface (1-2 minutes). Roll occasionally. Remove from potatoes and sausage from pan and place on serving plate.
8. Add oil, if needed, to pan fry eggs to taste (1-2 minutes). Add to plate and enjoy!

Nutrition Information

Serving size: 1 cup (about 200 g)
Calories: 467
Total Fat: 39.2 g
Total Carbohydrate: 10.8 g
Sugars: 0.7 g
Protein: 18.5 g
Sodium: 749 mg

English Muffin (Paleo, Gluten-Free)

Yield: 1 serving

Ingredients

1/4 cup almond flour
1 Tablespoon coconut flour
1/4 teaspoon baking soda
A pinch of salt
1 pasture-raised egg
1/2 Tablespoon coconut oil
2 Tablespoons water
1/4 teaspoon cinnamon
1/2 Tablespoon maple syrup

Directions

1. Grease a microwave-safe bowl, mug, or ramekin.
2. In a bowl, combine almond flour, coconut flour, baking soda, and salt.
3. Whisk in remaining ingredients.
4. Transfer mixture into prepared container.
5. Microwave on High for 2 minutes.
6. Remove from container, slice in half, and toast in toaster until desired doneness.

Nutrition Information

Serving size: 1 muffin
Calories: 354
Total Fat: 26.6 g
Total Carbohydrate: 18.6 g
Sugars: 7.2 g
Protein: 13.3 g
Sodium: 683 mg

Fruity Flaxseed Smoothie (Gluten-Free, Vegan)

Yield: 1 serving

Ingredients
1 1/2 cups fresh or frozen fruit of choice, like strawberries, blueberries, and banana
2 Tablespoons flax seed meal
1 cup low-fat vanilla soy milk

Directions
Put ingredients in a blender and blend until smooth.

Nutrition Information

Serving size: 1 1/2 cups
Calories: 330
Total Fat: 11 g
Total Carbohydrate: 52 g
Sugars: 24 g
Protein: 11 g
Sodium: 95 mg

Granola Mug (Gluten-Free, Vegan)

Yield: 1 serving

Ingredients
2 teaspoons water
2 teaspoon coconut oil
A pinch fine sea salt
A pinch of cinnamon
1/3 cup old-fashioned gluten-free rolled oats
1 Tablespoon chopped walnuts, almonds, or pecans

Ingredients (continued):

1 Tablespoon dried cranberries, raisins, or chopped dates
1 teaspoon sunflower seeds (optional)

Directions

1. Mix all ingredients EXCEPT dried cranberries together in a microwave-safe mug
2. Microwave at 50% power for 2 minutes.
3. Remove from microwave and mix well,
4. Return to microwave and cook until oats are golden brown (about 2 minutes).
5. Add cranberries and let cool.

Nutrition Information
Serving size: 1/2 cup
Calories: 357
Total Fat: 13.8 g
Total Carbohydrate: 38.5 g
Sugars: 6.1 g
Protein: 13.3 g
Sodium: 157 mg

Green Smoothie (Gluten-Free, Vegetarian)

Yield: 2 servings

Ingredients
2 cups baby spinach, washed
1 cucumber, cut into chunks
2 ripe bananas, peeled and sliced
2 ripe pear or apple, peeled and cored
2 scoops whey protein (or veggie protein powder), vanilla or unflavored
Handful of ice cubes

Directions

1. Place everything except ice in a blender and mix.
2. Add ice cubes and blend to desired smoothness.

Nutrition Information

Serving size: 1 1/2 cups
Calories: 200
Total Fat: 0.8 g
Total Carbohydrate: 46 g
Sugars 19 g
Protein: 14 g
Sodium: 81 mg

Ham and Egg Bowl (Gluten-Free)

Yield: 1 serving

Ingredients
2 thin slices deli ham
1 egg, beaten
1 Tablespoon shredded Cheddar cheese
1 Tablespoon chopped tomato, onion, or frozen peas

Directions

1. Fit the ham slice over the bottom and sides of a microwave-safe small bowl.
2. Add egg and vegetable.
3. Microwave on HIGH for 30 seconds.
4. Stir the egg and return to microwave. Microwave again until egg is set; 30-45 seconds.
5. Sprinkle with cheese and serve warm. Add a side of fresh fruit, if desired.

Nutrition Information

Serving size: 1/3-1/2 cup
Calories: 133
Total Fat: 8 g
Total Carbohydrate: 4 g
Sugars: 1.7 g
Protein: 12 g
Sodium: 420 mg

Microwave Scrambled Egg Mug (Gluten-Free)

Yield: 1 serving

Ingredients
1 egg
1/2 teaspoon coconut oil
1 Tablespoon whole milk
Salt and pepper, to taste
Optional toppings: chopped green onion, chopped tomato, gluten-free grated cheese

Directions

1. In a microwave-safe mug, beat egg, oil and milk until light colored.
2. Cook in microwave for 30 seconds.
3. Remove from microwave and stir. Add desired toppings (if using) and sprinkle with salt and pepper.
4. Cook again for about 20-45 seconds, depending on microwave. Overcooking will result in an unappetizing crust.
5. Serve warm.

Nutrition Information

Serving size: 1 mug
Calories: 82
Total Fat: 5.3 g
Total Carbohydrate: 1.7 g
Sugars: 0 g
Protein: 6.9 g
Sodium: 77 mg

Power Chocolate Smoothie (Paleo, Gluten-Free)

Yield: 1 serving

Ingredients

1 small ripe banana
1 Tablespoon honey
1 Tablespoon almond butter
1 Tablespoon coconut oil
1 Tablespoon ground Chia seeds

Ingredients (continued):

1 Tablespoon grass-fed gelatin (collagen hydrolysate)
1 cup almond milk
1/2 cup brewed coffee, warm
1 Tablespoon organic cacao powder
Ice cubes

Directions

1. Place everything in a blender and blend to mix.
2. Add ice cube and blend to desired smoothness.

Nutrition Information

Serving size: 1 1/2 cup
Calories: 424
Total Fat: 28.9 g
Total Carbohydrate: 32.5 g
Sugars: 10.6 g
Protein: 14.1 g
Sodium: 195 mg

Quinoa Porridge with Fruit (Gluten-Free, Vegetarian)

Yield: 4 servings

Ingredients
1 cup precooked quinoa
1/2 cup almond milk
2 Tablespoons nut butter of choice (try almond or sunflower seed)
1/2 teaspoon vanilla extract
1 teaspoon honey
1/2 cup strawberries, quartered
1/2 cup raspberries
1/2 cup blueberries
1 handful of pomegranate seeds
1/3 cup sliced almonds, toasted

Directions

1. Cook according to packaging instructions (usually to rinse then boil and then let sit for about 7 minutes) but leave slightly under done. After about 5 minutes of soaking, drain out water. Keep quinoa in pot over low heat.
2. Add almond milk, nut butter and vanilla. Cook for 2 minutes with occasional stirring.
3. Add honey to taste and transfer to bowls
4. Top with fruit and sprinkle with sliced almonds.

Nutrition Information
Serving size: 1 1/2 cups
Calories: 351
Total Fat: 13.9 g
Total Carbohydrate: 49.3 g
Sugars: 13.2 g
Protein: 10.7 g
Sodium: 20 mg

Scrambled Tofu with Turmeric (Gluten-Free, Vegetarian)

Yield: 2 servings

Ingredients
2 1/2 cups package organic tofu, firm, drained and wiped dry
1 Tablespoon grapeseed oil for cooking
2 Tablespoons nutritional yeast
1 teaspoon turmeric powder
1/4 teaspoon cayenne pepper
Black pepper to taste
1/2 teaspoon fine sea salt
2 Tablespoons almond or coconut milk
1/2 baby spinach
1/2 cup cherry tomatoes
1 toasted slice gluten-free bread with avocado as spread (optional)

Directions

1. Cube or rough chop tofu and mash with a fork.
2. Heat oil in a large frying pan, over medium heat.
3. Add mashed tofu, nutritional yeast, turmeric, pepper, salt and milk into pan and cook, stirring frequently, for 3 minutes.
4. Stir in baby spinach.
5. If using cherry tomatoes, push the tofu-spinach mixture to one side to make space for tomatoes (or use a separate pan).
6. Sear tomatoes (about 1 minute).
7. Cover the pan and remove from heat. Let ingredients cook in residual (1 minute).
8. Serve with avocado toast, if desired.

Nutrition Information

Serving size: 1 1/2 cups (does not include avocado toast)
Calories: 271
Total Fat: 15.6 g
Total Carbohydrate: 9.5 g
Sugars: 3.5 g
Protein: 29.1 g
Sodium: 630 mg

Smoothie Bowl with Fruit (Vegetarian)

Yield: 1 serving

Ingredients
3/4 cup nonfat plain Greek yogurt
1/4 cup reduced-fat milk
1 teaspoon vanilla extract
1 1/2 cups fruits of choice (like mango, peach, raspberry, blueberry), in bite-size pieces

Ingredients (continued):

1 tablespoon toasted sliced almonds
1 tablespoon unsweetened coconut flakes, toasted
1 teaspoon chia seeds

Directions

1. Place yogurt, milk, and vanilla in blender and pulse until mixed.
2. Transfer into a bowl.
3. Top with fruit.
4. Sprinkle with almonds, coconut, and chia seeds.

Nutrition Information
Serving size: 2 1/2 cups
Calories: 374
Total Fat: 10 g
Total Carbohydrate 50 g
Sugars: 40 g
Protein: 24 g
Sodium: 94 mg

Spicy Scrambled Eggs with Dates (Paleo, Gluten-Free)

Yield: 1 serving

Ingredients
1 Tablespoon olive oil
1 Tablespoon onion, sliced very thinly (optional)
1/3 cup baby spinach leaves
2 large eggs, lightly beaten
3 dates, pitted and chopped
1/4 Teaspoon dried chili flakes, or to taste
A dash of cumin powder
Salt and pepper, to taste

Directions

1. Heat oil in frying pan over medium heat.
2. Add onion (if using) and sauté until fragrant (about 15 seconds).
3. Add spinach and cook, with stirring, until dark and wilted (about 40 seconds).
4. Add egg, dates, spices, salt and pepper.
5. Reduce heat and scramble eggs until soft set (3-5 minutes).

Nutrition Information
Serving size: one 2-egg portion
Calories: 341
Total Fat: 23.2 g
Total Carbohydrate: 20.9 g
Sugars: 16.7 g
Protein: 13.7 g
Sodium: 245 mg

Spinach Ricotta Scramble (Gluten-Free)

Yield: 1 serving

Ingredients
1 egg, beaten lightly
4 egg white, beaten lightly
3 Tablespoons ricotta cheese
Pinch of ground thyme (optional)
3/4 cup baby spinach
Black pepper, to taste
Non-stick cooking spray

Directions

1. Spray a pan with non-stick spray and heat over medium heat.
2. Scramble the egg and egg whites and season with thyme (if using).
3. Transfer to a plate and top with ricotta.
4. Place spinach in pan and stir fry until wilted.
5. Place spinach over ricotta and then season with black pepper.

Nutrition Information

Serving size: 1 cup
Calories: 202
Total Fat: 9 g
Total Carbohydrate: 4 g
Sugars: 0 g
Protein: 27 g
Sodium: 368 mg

Strawberry-Yogurt Waffles (Vegetarian)

Yield: 1 serving

Ingredients
2 frozen organic high-protein waffles (Kodiak is a good brand)
1/2 cup Greek yogurt, plain or vanilla
2/3 cup sliced strawberries or other berries of choice

Directions

1. Toast waffles to desired crispness.
2. Top one piece with strawberries and yogurt. Place second piece on top and add the rest of the strawberries and yogurt.

Nutrition Information
Serving size: 2 waffles
Calories: 292
Total Fat: 8 g
Total Carbohydrate: 35 g
Sugars: 24 g
Protein: 16.5 g
Sodium: 427 mg

Superfood Breakfast Bowl (Gluten-Free, Vegetarian)

Yield: 1 serving

Ingredients
1 Tablespoon ground flax seed
2 Tablespoons ground nuts of choice, like almonds, walnuts, pecans, or cashews
1 teaspoon unsweetened cocoa powder
1 cup plain yogurt
1/4 cup blueberries
2 Tablespoons dried goji berries
1/2 teaspoon ground cinnamon
1/2 teaspoon honey
1 scoop whey protein

Directions

1. Use a blender or coffee grinder to grind flaxseed and nuts (1 minute).
2. Mix ground nuts and cocoa powder together.
3. Add the rest of the ingredients, mixing well.

Nutrition Information
Serving size: 1 bowl
Calories: 377
Total Fat: 11.6 g
Total Carbohydrate: 43.8 g
Sugars: 38 g
Protein: 30.4 g
Sodium: 229 mg

Turkey and Cheese Scramble (Gluten-Free)

Yield: 1 serving

Ingredients

1 egg, beaten lightly
1 egg white, beaten lightly
1/2 cup cottage cheese
1/2 cup sliced deli turkey, chopped
Black pepper, to taste
Non-stick cooking spray

Directions

1. Spray a pan with non-stick spray and heat over medium heat.
2. Scramble the egg and egg whites.
3. Add cheese and turkey.
4. Stir and cook until set.
5. Season with black pepper.

Nutrition Information
Serving size: 1 1/2 cups
Calories: 236
Total Fat: 8 g
Total Carbohydrate: 6 g
Sugars: 0 g
Protein: 34 g
Sodium: 94 mg

Turkey Sausage, Egg, and Fruit (Paleo, Gluten-Free)

Yield: 1 serving

Ingredients
2 Tablespoons coconut oil
1/3 cup ground turkey, thawed
1 teaspoon maple syrup
Pinch of sage
Pinch of thyme
Salt and pepper, to taste
1 egg, beaten lightly
1/2 cup fruit of choice

Directions

1. Heat oil in a frying pan over medium heat.
2. Put ground turkey and maple syrup in a bowl.
3. Sprinkle with spices and season with salt and pepper.
4. Mix well.
5. Divide mixture into 2. Take half, shape into a ball and flatten into a patty. Place in pan. Repeat for remaining mixture.
6. Cook until patties are browned on both sides (about 3 minutes on each side).
7. While patties are cooking, make space in pan for egg.
8. Season egg and scramble (1 minute). Transfer to plate.
9. Add cooked patties to egg along with fruit.

Nutrition Information

Serving size: 1 plateful (2 patties, 1 scrambled egg + 1/2 cup fruit)
Calories: 451
Total Fat: 34.6 g
Total Carbohydrate: 13.7 g
Sugars: 9.3 g
Protein: 23.7 g
Sodium: 407 mg

Veggie Stir-Fry with Eggs (Paleo)

Yield: 1 serving

Ingredients

2 Tablespoons coconut oil
1 cup fresh or frozen vegetables of choice, cut into bite-sized pieces
2 pasture-raised eggs
Salt and pepper to taste
Balsamic vinegar (optional)
1/2 cup fresh or frozen mango chunks, strawberry or pineapple (optional side)

Directions

1. Heat the oil in a medium sautee pan on medium-high heat.
2. Add the vegetables and stir-fry until tender-crisp (4 - 5 minutes).
3. Add the eggs and and cook approx. 2 minutes. Turn eggs over and cook another 1-2 minutes to desired firmness/doneness.
4. Remove from heat.
5. Season with salt and pepper.
6. Drizzle veggies with balsamic vinegar, if desired.
7. Optional: Serve with fruit cubes on the side.

Nutrition Information (with optional fruit)

Serving size: 2 cups
Calories: 414
Total Fat: 23.6 g
Total Carbohydrate: 32.9 g
Sugars: 19.7 g
Protein: 15.8 g
Sodium: 459 mg

Zucchini Power Omelet (Paleo)

Yield: 1 serving

Ingredients
1 Tablespoon olive oil
1 small zucchini, sliced thinly
2 eggs, beaten
Pepper, to taste

Directions

1. Heat oil in a pan over medium heat.
2. Cook zucchini until tender (about 2 minutes). Spread out in pan.
3. Add beaten eggs and cook until eggs are set (about 3 minutes).
4. Sprinkle with pepper.

Nutrition Information
Serving size: 1 omelet
Calories: 426
Total Fat: 37.7 g
Total Carbohydrate: 6.2 g
Sugars: 2.7 g
Protein: 13.5 g
Sodium: 146 mg

ABOUT THE AUTHOR

Dan DeFigio is a well-known nutrition expert who has been featured on CNN's Fit Nation, The Dr. Phil Show, *SELF* Magazine, Readers Digest, Muscle & Fitness, Shape Magazine, and a host of other media outlets. Dan is the author of numerous books, and the founder of **BeatingSugarAddiction.com.**

More books by Dan DeFigio:

Beating Sugar Addiction For Dummies

Beach Games For Kids!

The Two Week Transformation

Princess Wiggly

Beyond Smoothies

Other books from IronRingPublishing.com

Visit **IronRingPublishing.com** to sign up for notifications of new releases, free books, and other special giveaways!

The Two Week Transformation – Lose a pants size in 2 weeks, guaranteed!

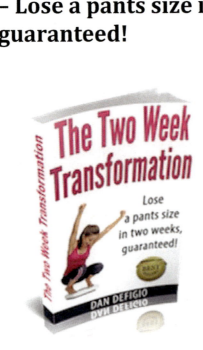

The Two Week Transformation is a simple, straightforward system that will start to change your body in just two weeks.

It's a simple guide that tells you exactly what to do for the next two weeks – what you should (and shouldn't) eat, recommended supplements, exercise tips, and some extra credit options too, if you really want to get serious.

If you follow ***The Two Week Transformation***, you're guaranteed to lose at least one pants size, and you will feel fantastic!

Here's why you'll love ***The Two Week Transformation***:

- It's an easy detox plan that DOESN'T involve complicated phases, measuring portions, or starving yourself
- You'll get proven nutrition secrets for maximum fat loss
- You'll be energized and feel great!
- You'll learn how to stop sabotaging yourself and finally find a way to lose weight quickly and easily

Get the kickstart you've been waiting for, and start your Two Week Transformation right now!

Available in paperback and Kindle formats, in both English and Spanish from IronRingPublishing.com.

Beyond Smoothies – Whey protein recipes that aren't smoothies!

If you're burned out on green smoothie recipes and juice detox diets, or you're looking for whey protein recipes that fit into a low-carb, high-protein diet, **Beyond Smoothies** is for you!

Fruit smoothies and protein shakes can get old fast. **Beyond Smoothies** comes to the rescue, delivering easy ways you can utilize nature's perfect protein that are far more interesting than boring fruit smoothie recipes!

Beyond Smoothies also uncovers the different types of whey protein, explains some of the many health benefits of using whey protein in your diet, and teaches you what kind of whey protein you should use.

Whether you're looking to get more protein in your diet, improve your health, lose weight, or supplement your detox diet, Beyond Smoothies will make it easy to add delicious ways to use whey protein.

Available in paperback and Kindle formats from IronRingPublishing.com.

Disclaimer and Terms of Use

The author and the publisher do not hold any responsibility for errors, omissions, or interpretation of the subject matter herein, and specifically disclaim any responsibility for the safety or appropriateness of any dietary advice or recipe preparation presented in this book. This book is presented for informational purposes only. Always consult a qualified health care practitioner before beginning any dietary regimen or before using any nutrition supplements.

© 2018 Iron Ring Publishing. All rights reserved

No part of this publication or the information it contains may be quoted, reused, transmitted, or reproduced in any form – electronic, mechanical, photocopy, recording, or otherwise – without prior written permission of the copyright holder.

Made in the USA
Middletown, DE
15 December 2018